Praise for Books  h

Journey Home
*Jennifer Kavanagh is a good narrator, she takes us
to the heart of what matters in so many lives.*

The World is our Cloister
*One would have to be spiritually dead not to find a very great
deal here which is worth reading - and putting into practice.*

A Little Book of Unknowing
*She continues in her books to nourish both the spirit
and the ever inquisitive mind with ease and panache.*

Small Change, Big Deal
*Read this book if you care about world and
UK poverty and want to be inspired!*

The Failure of Success
*A truly all-pervading sense of decency
and honesty permeates the book.*

Simplicity Made Easy
Jennifer writes beautifully and clearly

The Emancipation of B
This is one of the most original books I've ever read.

Heart of Oneness

Oneness

a little book of connection

Heart of Oneness
a little book of connection

Jennifer Kavanagh

CHRISTIAN
ALTERNATIVE

Winchester, UK
Washington, USA

First published by Christian Alternative Books, 2017
Christian Alternative Books is an imprint of John Hunt Publishing Ltd.,
Laurel House, Station Approach,
Alresford, Hants, SO24 9JH, UK
office1@jhpbooks.net
www.johnhuntpublishing.com
www.christian-alternative.com

For distributor details and how to order please visit the 'Ordering' section on our website.

Text copyright: Jennifer Kavanagh 2016

ISBN: 978 1 78535 685 8
978 1 78535 686 5 (ebook)
Library of Congress Control Number: 2017932883

A CIP catalogue record for this book is available from the British Library.

Design: Stuart Davies

Printed and bound by CPI Group (UK) Ltd, Croydon, CR0 4YY, UK

We operate a distinctive and ethical publishing philosophy in all areas of our business, from our global network of authors to production and worldwide distribution.

CONTENTS

References in the text are to books listed in Further Reading. When there is more than one work by the same author, they are distinguished in textual references by their date of publication.

1

Introduction

Sometimes we despair. Our screens and newspapers are full of violent images: bombed villages, random killings, the wilful destruction of precious historic sites – these are all expressions of man's inhumanity to man.

We live in a divided world. Human beings struggle to live together. Whether at the level of family, community, nation or world, we row, we fight, we kill each other. Communities are riven by racial, political and religious divisions. Conflict is part of the human condition, and it is all too often expressed in violence. Our world is full of poverty, inequality and injustice. Fear, greed, power-seeking and desperate need turn fellow human beings against each other and blind us to our common humanity.

This is a reality of which we are fully aware.

At times of political turmoil and humanitarian crisis it is all the more important to hold fast to the core values that define us as human beings and as part of something far beyond us. We need to remember that alongside the horrors there exists a parallel reality: of compassion, love, daily acts of kindness and selflessness, expressions of what we know in our hearts to be true: our essential interconnectedness. Most of the ills of the world stem from our departure from this reality.

There has always been a tension between the individual and community, between individual countries and attempts to bring them together. Conquering, empire-building and imposing a colonial power have made way for more subtle forms of power-mongering, but also to more collaborative unions. Over the past century we have seen the establishment of the United Nations, the Commonwealth, and a number of regional groups focused on trade or self-defence. At the same time there is a desire for separation: peoples such as the Basques rebel against what they regard as artificial borders and push for recognition as a separate entity. In recent years and months we have seen a stronger drive towards Scottish independence, and the UK's vote to leave the European Union.

We live in a paradoxical world. We are always alone and, whether we acknowledge it or not, always in community. We are unique, and yet there's only a hair's breadth of DNA difference between us and, not only other humans, but other species. With about two million species so far discovered, the planet is unimaginably diverse, and yet it is one. In the variety of religions, at the mystic level it is united. And it is in the Divine, at the heart of the multitudes of creation, that unity can be found. It is this series of paradoxes that this book will seek to address.

Life at each moment encompasses...both self and environment of all sentient beings in every condition of life as well as insentient beings—plants, sky and earth, on down to the most minute particles of dust (Nichiren, in Pearce).

2

A divided world

No man is an island,
Entire of itself,
Every man is a piece of the continent,
A part of the main.
If a clod be washed away by the sea,
Europe is the less.
As well as if a promontory were.
As well as if a manor of thy friend's
Or of thine own were:
Any man's death diminishes me,
Because I am involved in mankind,
And therefore never send to know for whom the bell tolls;
It tolls for thee.
(John Donne, 1572-1631)

It was in the year of 9/11 that I set off with my then partner for a year's backpacking round the world. Everywhere we went, there was an uncomfortable sense of a divided world, with its coexistent wealth and poverty. The divisions were highlighted by the attacks on the World Trade Centre, which took place just as we left the USA. In the previous months, as we travelled through Southern and then Central America, the influence of the US was everywhere to be seen, and resentment sometimes expressed. At one café in Brazil, a man leant over to our table and asked a question that fifteen years on has a renewed relevance, "Why are you Brits always hanging on to the coat-tails of America?"

Soon after our journey I wrote:

It was a strange year in which to travel: a time in which the relation of one country to another, and particularly between those in the developed world and those which are developing, were more acutely focused. I had not wanted to spend time in developed countries, but, on looking back, I can see that it was valuable to experience views from different countries and to carry messages from one to another. We are one world, and we all have responsibilities towards each other.

The sense of a divided world is not only between countries, but within them. We are well aware of the huge differences in wealth between countries. Those of us who live comfortable lives in largely affluent countries may be conscious of our good fortune. We know how much poverty there is the world, of the vast differences between one country and another. We have been less conscious of the inequality within countries although, with the growth of food banks in rich Western countries, our awareness is perhaps growing too.

We live in a world beset by inequality and injustice. The horrors of the trans-Atlantic slave trade may be over but, although slavery is no longer legal, the practice is widespread in many parts of the world, including in the West where people are trafficked to be sex or domestic slaves or indentured labourers. Even within legal parameters, inequality and ill-treatment are rife, especially in the treatment of those with less power: those in lower positions in a hierarchy, such as children or old people.

Over recent decades much progress in social equality has been made, for instance, in the fields of gender, race and sexuality, but much remains to be done. In some countries child labour is still commonplace, and homosexuality a crime punishable by death. Apartheid in South Africa and segregation in the USA are still in very recent memory, and it takes generations for any profound change to take effect. Indeed, as I write, recent advances in inclusive legislation in the USA are being brutally reversed. And the public need for scapegoats continues. Over recent years, there has built up in the UK an unprecedented alliance between government of both main parties and the right-wing press, to demonise groups of people who are already marginalised, such as homeless people, prisoners and those seeking asylum.

In their ground-breaking book, *The Spirit Level*, epidemiologists Kate Pickett and Richard Wilkinson present stark evidence of the impact that inequality within countries has on those countries and those who live there. Taking twenty-three of the richest countries (excluding tax havens) and forty US States, they measured the different levels of inequality within each, and the impact of that inequality. Using the 20:20 ratio measure of income inequality from the UN Development Programme Human Development indicators for the years 2003-6, they uncover the stark contrast between material success and social failure. In every indicator: life expectancy, maths and literacy, infant mortality, homicides, imprisonment, teenage births, trust, obesity, mental illness (including drug and alcohol addiction) and social mobility, the most unequal countries – topped by the USA, with the UK in third place - have the highest levels of disadvantage. The subtitle of their book is "Why Equality is Better for Everyone".

On our doorstep

One of my very first memories is of hearing on the news how children were starving in Ethiopia. I turned to my parents in distress: "If people are starving, why can't we put tins of food on a boat and send them to them?" The answer I was given, of course, was that it wasn't as simple as that. The general feeling, as I was growing up, was that poverty and injustice were just too big, that there was nothing that we could do.

It was not until the mid-1990s that I realised that it was possible to see the world in a different way, and that poverty and disadvantage are not just "out there" but on our own doorstep. What opened my eyes to the reality of 1990s Britain and the prejudices and preconceptions in my own life was being asked to co-ordinate a series of tea runs for homeless people. I was working in publishing; I had never volunteered in my life, and knew nothing of street homelessness. So, to educate myself, I went on a tea run. I was nervous: sure that I would either be sneered at or hit over the head by a bottle-wielding druggie. Of course neither happened. Instead, as I walked over to a young man in a sleeping bag and asked if he would like a cup of tea or coffee, and whether he took sugar, I found myself forming a relationship with another human being. Instead of passing by a bundle in a doorway with embarrassment and guilt, I was doing something, however small, and my preconceptions fell away. It was an epiphany, and I realised in that moment that that bundle in the doorway could have been me.

I learned so much that night and on the nights that followed. We are privileged to touch people at a time in their lives when, stripped of everything but the essentials, they often seem more in touch with what matters. Although, of course, I would not wish poverty on anyone, we have so much to learn from those who have least. Anything we give is repaid a hundred-fold.

What I learnt from those encounters with homeless people was something that has remained with me in later work - with prisoners, asylum seekers and women in rural Africa. It is something that is easy to know in our heads, but needs to be known viscerally and in our hearts. I now understand how completely we are one in our human predicament.

It was as a result of that experience that in my year's travels and also for subsequent work in South Africa and Ghana it has felt important to distance myself as little as possible from the people I am with. Travelling on local transport, being in touch with how local people live, is for me a crucial factor. When finding myself with rich relations in Guatemala or in a smart hotel in Eastern Cape, I felt a dis-comfort, an un-ease. In emails to friends I struggled to explain that my response was not a rationalised or willed feeling that this way of life was inappropriate but – rather to my surprise – that I felt I was in the wrong place. Yes, I am white, foreign and fortunate, but in working with people who have fewer choices, I want to be alongside, to live as much as possible – if only for that brief time – in a simpler way.

What I realise from my experiences with those living different lives, those who have fewer choices than my own, is that separating ourselves, keeping at a distance from others, blinding ourselves to the impact of our lives on others in the world, allows even those of us of good will to lead lives that are destructive to others.

Why is this? Maybe we have to look at not only what is on our own doorstep but in our own hearts and behaviour.

Preconceptions and prejudice

We all have preconceptions: we all make assumptions about the people we meet, based on superficial factors. Walking down the street, we draw conclusions from the way people walk, dress and speak. Why do we do it? In part, it is a response to the complexity of the world and our busy lives: it is quicker and easier to lump people together, to put them into pigeonholes. Acting on these assumptions, however, can be dangerous. It can result in stereotyping, which in turn can lead to the belittling and marginalisation of others.

And the divisions in our society are all too visible. The recent rise of prejudice and scapegoating, bolstered by right-wing parties and press, has led to the marginalisation of homeless people, and the expression of prejudice against those coming from other countries, or of other faiths. Racism, sexism and homophobia, although less accepted than a generation ago, are often not far below the surface, and in some quarters have recently erupted in a shockingly blatant way. The news is full of examples of verbal abuse, bullying or more extreme forms of violence towards those on the margins or perceived as different.

In some media the words "migrant" and "Muslim" have become terms of abuse.

When we know someone, our responses are different. When a generalisation is made, and we remind the speaker that their grandson is gay or their best friend's husband is black, the response is invariably "Oh, of course, I don't mean him."

One day, when I complained to a friend: "Oh, Fred is so sexist", he responded: "Oh, he's everything-ist. Don't take it personally." And it's true, on the whole, that when prejudice takes root, it spreads to cover anyone whose difference feels threatening: whether in race, sexuality or gender. Discrimination is part of a general attitude that seeks to exclude any individual or group that is perceived as different from the social norm.

Why do we feel so threatened by difference? What are our barriers to connection? Fear, greed and lack of self-esteem all have their part to play. Otherness is often projected on to those who are closest (for instance between Arab and Jew, Hutus and Tutsis). My fellow-feeling with the bundle sleeping in a doorway has led me to an understanding that our need to scapegoat those on the margins of society stems from a *fear* that it might be us. The fact that we single out homeless people, those with mental health problems or prisoners is that we know, all too well, that it could be us. Pushing them away expresses our wish to distance ourselves from that possibility.

Anyone who has to attack another in order to feel right about him or herself has no clue who and what they truly are. They believe...that their worth and their power arise from their ability to dominate or even destroy another. Blinded to their own divine nature, they cannot see the divine nature of those around them. Oblivious to the reality of oneness, they do not comprehend that when they attack another it is themselves they attack (Pearce).

How can we respond to those exhibiting prejudice and exclusion?

> As healers, our task is to witness to the truth of who they are. We don't condone their actions or defend their ignorance, but we hold to the truth of what they cannot see: that in their essence they are whole, and far more beautiful than they imagine. Because we are all one, and in the peace of your mind, I find my peace. As you realize your divinity, I am more able to see my own.
>
> ...There is no such thing as separateness. We are in this together, and together is what we are here to learn (*ibid.*).

And, when a world event leaps out of the news to catch our attention, togetherness can be very powerfully expressed. The rise of social media has enabled remarkable efforts to effect change: thousands of pounds are raised through crowdfunding, and a viral tweet can alert us to a situation that moves thousands of people unknown to each other to unite over a common cause. *"Je suis Charlie"* was an expression of world-wide solidarity for those killed in the attack on the satirical magazine *Charlie Hebdo* on 7 January 2015, and more generally for the freedom of the press. As attacks hit other places, the movement expanded to include, for instance, Brussels and Orlando. *"Je suis Bruxelles"*, *"Je suis Orlando"*. The danger is that such mass waves of solidarity can too easily exclude those from less familiar places, and critics of the partiality of our support have posted *"Je suis"* Baghdad, Istanbul, every place where the scale of atrocity has shocked us into action.

> When we stand in solidarity with those being targeted we assert the reality that there is no "other." When any of us is injured we are all injured. When any of us is targeted, we are all targeted. Practicing solidarity, we become with-standers,

not bystanders, demonstrating the truth that separateness does not exist. (*ibid.*)

We have to be careful. Mass movements such as these can also lead to a rather random demonising of anyone who disagrees, anyone bearing a different label, leading in its turn to further conflict.

* * *

One of the results of our polarised world and one of the greatest challenges to the expression of our love of our fellow human beings, to our sense of oneness, is our response to the refugee crisis. At last Europe has been brought face to face with the vast scale of displacement, something that has been apparent to other continents for a very long time. It is no longer possible to ignore the reality of those millions of threatened lives: the desperation that will lead people to risk their lives to find sanctuary, the conditions in which refugees find themselves once they arrive, and the callousness with which they are often treated, the length that most governments of rich countries will go to shore up their borders to keep them out.

No one wants to be a refugee. Those of us who live settled lives, who have not lived through war or oppression, can have little idea of the turmoil, the violent uprooting, displacement causes. In facing this reality, we are pressed to accept our responsibility as fellow human beings.

Western countries have a distorted view of their own generosity. Contrary to popular belief, it is developing countries, with the majority of their own people living in extreme poverty, which are host to the largest number of refugees. People leaving extreme hardship, war or abuse will move either to the nearest country that will accept them, in the hopes of a quick return, or to countries where there are family ties. The view of many countries that people fleeing their homes, for whatever reason, head for rich countries in the West is simply not true.

In Europe, the last few decades have seen an increasingly draconian attitude to those seeking asylum. There has developed a culture of disbelief that has led to acute xenophobia in some quarters, and increased levels of destitution among asylum seekers. A report by the Council of Europe has attributed blame for the increase in racism in the UK to increasingly restrictive asylum and immigration laws.

And both the situation and our response to it have deteriorated. According to the UN High Commissioner for Refugees (UNHCR), in 2015 there were an estimated 59.5 million people displaced worldwide, and 86% of the world's refugees are hosted by developing countries. Once again those who have least are shaming the rest of us; they are showing us the way.

But even as a wave of xenophobia sweeps through Europe and parts of the United States, there are small chinks of light. European governments may vary in their responses; the tabloid press and the right wing may want to express suspicion of anyone seeking sanctuary and urge us to hug our riches and freedom to ourselves, but among the public there is a groundswell of good will, of people welcoming refugees, sponsoring their admission, sending donations and volunteering for refugee centres. The campaigning organisation Citizens UK is asking local councils to sign up to welcome fifty refugees each.

The City of Sanctuary movement, which began in Britain in 2005, aims to build a culture of hospitality for people seeking sanctuary in the UK, to create a network of towns and cities throughout the country which are proud to be places of safety for people seeking sanctuary and helping them integrate into their local communities. Since then, the organisation has supported the development of over forty City of Sanctuary initiatives in towns and cities across UK and Ireland. We want to make a difference.

In 2017, the presidential executive ban on people from various Muslim countries entering the USA and the suspension of the refugee programme were met by massive public protest. The strength of feeling against exclusion and division were marked by thousands marching and demonstrating on the streets of American, British and European cities, proclaiming our support for refugees, "We welcome refugees", "We stand together against hate".

* * *

What I was told as a child does not have to be true. We are not as powerless as most of us believe. In coming across Quakers I discovered a group who are making a difference, in small, local ways, perhaps, but it showed that it was possible to do something. Despite its small size, the Religious Society of Friends (Quakers) has been prominent in social reform: in prisons, against slavery and at the beginnings of, for instance, Amnesty International and Oxfam. It's about taking responsibility. If not me, then who? God has no other hands but ours.

The more I looked, the more I discovered that everywhere in the world, people of all faiths and none are making a difference, and this discovery was hugely empowering - I began to believe that I too might make a contribution.

Working as a volunteer has taught me that it is as much about how we work as what we do. The former Dominican priest, Matthew Fox, expressed his shock at discovering a statement in a recent edition of the Oxford English Dictionary that the definition of compassion as a relation among equals is "obsolete" and that it is about superior/inferior relationships. Such a reduction of a complex and mutual relationship to one between subject and object is so far from the truth. It is the patronising top-down approach of "do-gooding" that is obsolete. Exercising compassion is not about something we do *to* people, or even *for* people, but *with* people. It's about relationship, working alongside, and recognising the mutual benefit.

There is no dividing line between giver and receiver. My need allows your compassion to flower. My gratitude gives your life meaning and purpose, and so the gift, the giver and the receiver become a Circle of Blessing (Carolyn Fletcher in the *Friend*, 25 November 2016).

Even better than recognising our mutual benefit is acknowledging our own place in something, accepting that we ourselves are in need of help. It is not just about "them"; it is about us too.

The Alternatives to Violence programme (AVP) is one of the most inclusive programmes I know. Facilitators don't just deliver a programme; in each workshop we learn alongside each other. And in fourteen years of facilitating workshops I continue to learn, from the programme itself, and from the wide variety of participants. Dealing better with conflict is something that we all need to do. In fact, if I have a criticism, at least of how we do it in the UK (it may be different elsewhere), it is that we have a patronising attitude to our client base. Apart from those in prison, we invariably target people with other labelled issues - mental health, homelessness, the most disadvantaged. Whereas, if we ask who demonstrates the most adversarial way of dealing with conflict, surely we should be focusing on politicians and lawyers: those whose highly visible ways of working could be transformed, and bring that transformation to others.

AVP includes an exercise called "In Common", in which people get into pairs to discuss what they have in common, then join up with another pair, then fours join up until the whole group has found things that they have in common – usually, by that stage, fundamental things such as the need for love and the love of the sky and the stars. In doing this exercise with young offenders, I could see that that even in widely different circumstances we still have some of the same struggles. It is to recognise our common humanity.

3

It's a small world

Relation is the essence of everything that exists (Eckhart)

It may be a divided world, but it is also a small one. In a global society, we are more informed than ever about what is happening in the rest of the world; we are more and more connected. In our constant use of email, social media and the World Wide Web, distance shrinks. But our connection as human beings is both more ancient and more profound than that facilitated by our electronic media.

Our lives are peopled. However much an outsider we may feel, however isolated we are, whether we live alone or with others, we are part of community, related by blood and genes, linked by occupation or by neighbourhood. When participants in a workshop are asked what communities they belong to, their answers fill several sides of flip-chart paper: anything from bell-ringing to a golf club; from the local neighbourhood to religious affiliation; from Facebook to a reading group.

Human beings are rooted in community: family, neighbourhood and nation. We may feel that we don't belong or may be part of an inward-looking clan, tribe, or even closed society. But community is not just a group of like-minded individuals. It includes those whom we dislike or those with whom we disagree. It includes the prisoner, the recent arrival and the bad-tempered man next door. Even shut behind gates or fences, we cannot hide the fact that we are dependent on circles of humanity: the postman, the plumber, the farmer, possibly in another country, who produced our food, the manufacturers who made our furniture and clothes – almost certainly from another country. In a welfare state we recognise our mutual responsibilities. We pay taxes not just for our own benefit, but for the rest of the community.

Sometimes we acknowledge our connection. A meeting at a bus stop may result in eye contact, a smile, a comment about a common cause - the weather or late running of a bus - or a full-blown conversation exploring a little of each other's lives and views, and a reluctant parting. In an ocean of separateness we experience a drop of connection.

Or we may not. We are not always in the mood for openness, and nor are others. There are times of reflection or vulnerability when we need our solitude. We need to be sensitive to the needs of others. And to what is appropriate. When my son and I got on a tube together a few years ago, he muttered that the two men opposite were not those with whom eye contact would be a good idea. He had an intuition of danger, and an instinct for self-protection.

But, on the whole, people are more willing - even eager - for connection than we expect, even in large cities like London which are considered "unfriendly". Enjoying the balance of anonymity and community, both locally and on a wider scale, I have never found it so. Connection often fails through a lack of awareness. When people are made aware of something, they often spring into action, giving directions, giving up a seat for one less able, or helping to carry luggage up the stairs.

Indeed, the daily dance as we weave our way along city pavements and in other public spaces shows that, on the whole and with notable exceptions, we have cultivated an awareness of others' need for space, making way, as needed, for a pushchair, a ladder or someone on crutches. This dance becomes one-sided when confronted by those who walk with mobile phones, and I have long fantasised about having a separate pavement lane for those. Preferably, it would be two-way, so that phone walkers would have to negotiate with each other!

In fact, the thousands of people on their mobile phones on the bus or walking down the street are in fact demonstrating their need to feel connected. But by confining their communication to someone elsewhere they are limiting their awareness of those physically near them, closing off the possibility of a wider connection.

A feeling of closeness can go beyond family or those that we call friends, those with whom we have had a long association. John O'Donohue writes beautifully about the deep connection we can feel with another even when we meet for the first time:

There are some people in your life with whom you felt a wonderful affinity the moment you met them. The more they told you, the more you felt as if they were talking from a common world you had somehow secretly shared before you ever came to know each other. Within the newly discovered affinity, so much can be assumed and intuited. Nothing needs to be said, tested or proved. You sense each other's spirit and in some inexplicable way, you do know each other. Trust is not a question; you settled into an embrace of belonging that seemed to have always held you (2004:144).

There are times when we feel related to others, even those we have never met.

Field

Many of us have occasional experiences of a connection of which the rest of the time we are barely conscious. It's something that we might crudely call telepathy, but is at a level well beyond party tricks. An example is a Quaker Meeting for Worship, which is a collective experience, a waiting on God, and many say that the more conscious we are of the others in the room, the deeper the worship will be. Frequently when someone stands up to speak of what is on their mind, it echoes what has been in the heart of others in the room; on many occasions I have thought of speaking, when someone has stood and expressed better than I could what I was thinking.

Clown and storyteller, Angela Halvorson-Bogo, refers to something she calls the field between us, which, if made a focus for a group performance or during Skype or virtual group meditation, deepens the experience. Tuning in to others who are meditating or praying at that moment in other parts of the world creates a field, an inner community. I like the idea of us all as charged particles, creating an electric, psychic or mystic field. The closer we are, the stronger the field.

John O'Donohue writes of "the subtle world between things":

Between every separate thing, beneath the slow time-film that rolls forth each day and night, in the cold unknown between strangers, in the limbo land of numbed indifference and even in the vast distance between centuries and their lost memory, there exists another world, an invisible world where all this distance and separation is embraced ...The space between seems empty to the eye yet to the imagination it is vibrant with pathways towards beauty. Divine space has a latent grandeur (2004:242).

This space between things is indeed not empty. From it may emerge creative ideas that seem to have come out of nowhere: ideas that are almost literally "in the air". As individuals, seemingly working in isolation in different parts of the world, come up with the same scientific discovery or idea for a biographical study, they are in grace-filled receipt of an idea whose time has come.

When we become aware of it, it is this mysterious kind of connection which can provide active guidance. Synchronicity is a seeming coincidence - a phone call, a piece on the radio - that confirms a course of action. Listening out for such synchronicities can become a form of decision-making. One of my friends goes so far as to say that he is disappointed when he becomes aware of a synchronicity: the connection has been there all the time, and he has only just become aware of it. For many, God is connection, relationship, the linking factor in all living beings.

If we believe in an underlying connectivity, the power of positive thinking, intercessionary prayer, being held "in the Light", may not seem so far-fetched. People report again and again a feeling of being upheld, prayed for, and how it has helped. But, even when people don't know they are being prayed for, some research seems to indicate that prayer has an impact; conditions often improve. And, as always, the experience seems to be mutually beneficial.

Generations

Our oneness as human beings is not only "horizontally" across space, but also "vertically", across time. Through genes and memory we are one with those who have gone before, and those who are to come. Indigenous cultures have long pointed the way to what some would consider our responsibility to the legacy of our forefathers. "Community", says Matthew Fox, "embraces the ancestors" (2000:89).

Even more, there is a sense of responsibility to those who are to come: those whose lives will be impacted by our own behaviour. How we treat the planet, the state that we leave the world in, will be the inheritance of our children, grandchildren and beyond. Our responsibility to the future is well understood by Native Americans who, in taking every important decision, consider its impact on the seventh generation. Neale Donald Walsche considers that "your heirs stand beside you, watching your decisions on their behalf" (298).

But our relationship is not only with those we recognize as blood relations. We are connected more extensively than we realise. The popularity of genealogy has grown over recent decades, and the advent of the internet has made family research much easier. However, few of us know the history of our families further back than a few generations, and at each generation, we generally trace only one or two of the multiple threads of kinship. In the late 1990s, mathematical models calculated that the commonality of our ancestry was far more recent than we had previously thought and a few years ago, Peter Ralph and Graham Coop, using genome-wide data from European individuals, proved the accuracy of these calculations. Going back only 600 years, the common ancestry of Europeans can be traced back to a single individual. And only a thousand years ago, the common ancestry of every individual European can be traced in a startling criss-cross of connection.

Even with what we already know, few of us can trace the same nationality back on both sides of our family for many generations. I am half Russian; the English side includes injections of Portuguese and French. In recent times, members of my family have married people of Irish, Guatemalan, Swiss, Colombian and Malay nationalities. If I were to take a DNA test, I'd probably discover an even richer heritage. Apparently, every European has Viking and Jewish blood in them. Scientifically, it would seem, race is meaningless, and any discrimination completely without foundation.

Only Us

Last year, a friend of mine, an Anglican chaplain in a psychiatric hospital, set up a mental health campaign called Only Us; there is no "they"; there is only us. Increasingly we are beginning to understand that the state of our mental health is on a spectrum: whether we are referring to conditions of autism, bipolarity or depression.

But the concept is not restricted to mental health issues. The same phrase, the same principle, applies to all aspects of our existence. In terms of nationality, ability, race, gender, age, sexual orientation, whether housed or homeless, indigenous or a refugee, pigeonholing simply doesn't work. In terms of sexual orientation, there are many nuances of difference. There is no such thing as the other - whatever labels we try to attach to people: there is only us. And God in us.

Ubuntu is an ancient African word meaning not only compassion but "I am what I am because of who we all are". We are one. As John O'Donohue says, "We are a family of the one presence".

And "only us" includes more than people.

4

Universe

Every moment we live in split-second reality
as unique and simultaneous truths. We are one
and together because of each other,
with each other,
for each other.
(From "Turning on the Light" by Gunilla Norris)

The natural world is an extraordinary model of oneness, not only in the relationship between individual beings but as a whole. Not for nothing is it called a universe, from the Latin: *universus* – whole, combined into one.

That oneness is expressed in the overwhelming inter-relatedness of all that exist within it. Examples of mutuality and interdependence not only within but between species are all around us. Insects feed on nectar and carry pollen from one flower to another; the seeds of many plants are dispersed by ants. As salmon go to the ocean, they collect nutrients by feeding, and eventually return nutrients to the streams, supplying muchneeded food for numerous animals and plants, which in turn provide food for the salmon fry the following year. Even nonaquatic organisms benefit from the nutrients salmon bring upstream. Not only that, but after spawning, most salmon die, thus providing a food source for otters, eagles and bears before winter sets in. Without this nutrition, there would be a severe drop in the population of these animals. In life and in death, the salmon provide for others.

Ecologist Peter Wohlleben writes of a famous example of the impact of the behaviour that different species have on each other, an example that reveals the fine balance of the natural world.

Wolves disappeared from Yellowstone... Park, in the 1920s. When they left, the entire ecosystem changed. Elk herds in the park increased their numbers and began to make quite a meal of the aspens, willows, and cottonwoods that lined the streams. Vegetation declined and animals that depended on the trees left.

When the wolves returned, seventy years later,

The wolf packs kept the herds on the move, browsing diminished, and the trees sprang back. The roots of cottonwoods and willows once again stabilised stream banks and slowed the flow of water. This, in turn, created space for animals such as beavers to return... The wolves turned out to be better stewards of the land than people, creating conditions that allowed the trees to grow and exert their influence on the landscape. (xi-xii)

Invisible connection

Such visible connections are clear, but other examples of the relationship between species are less familiar. The astonishing interconnectedness of the natural world is all around us. And not only around us, but beneath our feet. Much of the web of connection in the natural world is invisible to our eyes: some because it is too minute to be seen, but mostly because it occurs underground, inside the bodies of other species, or in other processes that can't be seen.

Take mushrooms. Recently I was given a lift from Mallaig to Fort William by someone who turned out to be a mycologist. On that two-hour journey across the glorious Scottish landscape, I learned of the marvel that is fungal connectedness.

What we generally know and see of fungi is a tiny part of their existence. Underground is a mass of branching, thread-like hyphae, the vegetative part of a fungus called mycelium which enable the mushroom to feed. And not only feed, but exchange nutrients with its neighbours. A single mycelium can cover thousands of acres and last for thousands of years.

Most plants form a relationship with fungi through their roots, which absorb water, nitrogen and phosphorus in exchange for sugar. The result is not only healthier plants and fungi, but a healthier soil too. According to Nic Fleming, on the BBC Earth website,

> The more we learn about these underground networks, the more our ideas about plants have to change. They aren't just sitting there quietly growing. By linking to the fungal network they can help out their neighbours by sharing nutrients and information – or sabotage unwelcome plants by spreading toxic chemicals through the network.

Trees, it seems, also connect with others through their root systems either directly, by intertwining their roots, or indirectly, by growing fungal networks around the roots that serve as a sort of extended nervous system connecting separate trees. If this weren't remarkable enough, these arboreal mutualities are even more complex - trees appear able to distinguish their own roots from those of other species and even of their own relatives. (https://www.brainpickings.org/2016/09/26/the-hidden-life-of-trees-peter-wohlleben/)

Trees and mushrooms: these are beings that we can see, even if their means of connection are under the earth. But there is a vast number of beings that are invisible to the naked eye. Microbes have had a bad press, but despite the best known being the bacteria that infect our bodies with disease, most microbes are in fact benign. In his fascinating book, *I Contain Multitudes*, Ed Jong reveals to us this hidden world.

The Earth contains a variety of different ecosystems:

rainforests, grasslands, coral reefs, deserts, salt marches, each with its own particular community of species. But a single animal is full of ecosystems too. Skin, mouth, gut, genitals, and organ that connects with the outside world: each has its characteristic community of microbes (4).

Microbes, he tells us, are everywhere and in astonishing numbers – an estimated hundred trillion inhabit every human being, helping us digest our food, and build and shape our organs. According to Yong, every aspect of our bodies is touched by the microbes we contain, and we reap the rewards of a harmonious relationship with them in "ecological opportunities and the accelerated pace with which we can grasp them" (264). For microbes are not only present in our bodies; we transfer them to and receive them from other beings as we move through the world, eating, breathing and touching as we go. They form part of our connection to the wider world.

Yong goes on to compare a diseased gut with a dying coral reef, saying that in each case it is a matter of "the balance of organisms" going "awry". The microbes might be different for different species but, says Yong, "the same principles govern our alliances" (4). "We cannot fully understand the lives of animals without understanding microbes and our symbioses with them." This is an astounding revelation of an invisible yet globally overarching community.

These examples demonstrate not only the ability of species to add to our environment, but even to correct or heal damage that has been done. It is not what they "should" be doing but just what, in their very nature, they do. How they are.

The connectedness of the universe extends even, we learn, to the sounds of its individual beings. There is not only a collective presence but a collective voice. Bernie Krause is a sound engineer. He moved from making recordings that formed the soundtrack of many bestselling films to developing a passion for recording the natural world. Tiring of the artificial isolating of individual species, he has specialised in the collective sound-scape of creation: the interweaving of all sounds of the natural world. In his book, *The Great Animal Orchestra*, he writes of geophany – the sound of inanimate natural powers such as the wind and water - and biophany: the sounds of living creatures, each pitched at an appropriate time and level of pitch, vibration and dynamic for its habitat, whether in the forest or under the ocean.

Krause talks of how

creatures vocalise in distinctive kinship with each other, particularly in older, more stable habitats... In the healthiest of habitats, all of these sounds coalesce in an elegant web of organised signals that are full of information about each organism's relationship to the whole. From this ensemble comes the music of nature (88, 126).

This collective voice, according to him, "represents the oldest and most beautiful music on the planet" (220).

At an even more remote and mysterious level comes a connection known as quantum entanglement, which occurs when a pair of particles, such as photons, interact physically. A laser beam fired through a certain type of crystal can cause individual photons to be split into pairs of entangled photons, which remain connected so that actions performed on one affect the other, even when separated by hundreds of miles or even more. The phenomenon annoyed Albert Einstein so much that he called it "spooky action at a distance".

Trees, fungi, cells, protons and microbes, they're all at it. There is so much that we don't know about the universe that we live in, but what we can say with confidence is that built into its fabric is a web of connection. As Satish Kumar wrote,

Existence is an intricately interconnected web of relation-ships. We share the breath of life and thus we are connected. Whether we are rich or poor, black or white, young or old, humans or animals, fish or fowl, trees or rocks, everything is sustained by the same air, the same sunshine, the same water, the same soil. There are no boundaries, no separation, no division, no duality; it is all the dance of eternal life where spirit and matter dance together...The process of the universe is embedded in the life support system of mutuality.

Let us take note.

5

Human and other animals

We need another and a wiser and perhaps a more mystical concept of animals. Remote from universal nature, and living by complicated artifice, man in civilization surveys the creature through the glass of his knowledge and sees thereby a feather magnified and the whole image in distortion. We patronize them for their incompleteness, for their tragic fate of having taken form so far below ourselves. And therein we err and we greatly err. For the animal shall not be measured by man. in a world older and more complete than ours they move finished and complete, gifted with extensions of the senses we have lost or never attained, living by voices we shall never hear. They are not brethren, they are not underlings; they are other nations, caught with ourselves in the net of life and time, fellow prisoners of the splendor and travail of the earth.
(Henry Beston, quoted in Mitchell).

Our view of the rest of creation has traditionally been reflected in what we read in Genesis:

And God said, Let us make man in our image, after our likeness: and let them have dominion over the fish of the sea, and over the fowl of the air, and over the cattle, and over all the earth, and over every creeping thing that creepeth upon the earth. (Genesis I:26, KJV)

Many still believe that other beings are there for our use and delectation, that nonhuman animals are there for the use of humans - as food, beasts of burden or objects of experimentation in a process that Thomas Berry calls our "reduction of the entire universe to subservience to the human" (35).

Dr Les Mitchell talks about how the "life purposes" of various nonhuman animals are described solely in terms of their use to human beings: producing flesh or eggs for us to eat, or wool for us to use. Or in terms of their commercial value. Animals are even named according to anthropocentric purposes: pit pony, laboratory rat, war horse.

We may have left behind some of the worst excesses of our ill-treatment of nonhuman animals – bear baiting, butterflies pinned to a board – but we still have a way to go in examining our relationship with the animal world. There is still much ill-treatment. Although challenged, such practices as animal experimentation, fox hunting, battery chickens and mink farms still continue. Even if public opinion has turned against trophy hunters and the killing of beautiful animals, antlers still adorn the walls of baronial halls. And there is much more that is taken for granted, condoned even by those who believe themselves to be living compassionate lives. And we are biased: it is easier to relate to some animals than others. It is the beautiful animals – the pandas and lions – that catch our attention. The less obviously attractive are killed or ill-treated with impunity.

Although figures from the RSPCA demonstrate that cases of cruelty are relatively rare and it seems clear that people in the US and countries of the European Union do not, as a general principal, support the abuse of nonhuman animals, in the farming industry we seem to shut our eyes to their treatment. Les Mitchell quotes from section 959.13 of the State of Ohio animal cruelty statute: No one shall

> torture an animal, deprive one of necessary sustenance, unnecessarily or cruelly beat, needlessly mutilate or kill, or impound or confine an animal without supplying it during such confinement with a sufficient quantity of good wholesome food and water.

As he says, "What does it mean to *unnecessarily* beat, *cruelly* beat or *needlessly* mutilate?" Citing ignorance, justification or the perceived benefits of such acts, it is clear, as Mitchell says, that there is a degree of moral disengagement among consumers about the abuse to which animals are subjected. We too easily shut our eyes to the relationship between the chops on our plate and the lambs we see gambolling in the field. The sanitised pack of mince or chicken nuggets from the supermarket shelves give little reminder of the animals who have been killed to provide them. It was only the reality of seeing a beautiful array of fish flapping in a bucket, gasping for breath, that persuaded me to give up eating fish. I was not surprised to read that there is as much evidence that fish feel pain and suffer as there is for birds and mammals. Even those of us who avoid swatting a fly or treading on an ant conduct an unthinking lifestyle that causes immense suffering to other creatures.

But we all have to eat, and we make choices according to the needs of our specific bodies and our individual and cultural preferences. Allergies, intolerances and health issues will affect what we eat. Awareness of our interconnectedness and compassion towards our fellow beings will also affect our choices. Different cultures approve the eating of different animals. And respect can take many forms.

For Native Americans, it is natural to kill animals but traditionally in many tribes permission is first to be sought from the animal's spirit. Respect demands that the whole of the animal is used, whether for food, leather or other purposes. Only then can taking life be justified. These days, many other carnivores take care about the provenance of the meat, only buying from sources they know to be humane in their treatment of the animals.

Vegetarians choose not to eat meat or fish or products like gelatine made from them. Vegans also refuse to eat dairy products or eggs. Jainism prescribes *ahimsa* (non-violence) towards all living beings to the greatest possible extent so some Jains wear masks over their mouth and nose to avoid inadvertently harming insects or microbes by inhaling them, and brush the path before them so that they should not accidentally tread on any creature. They generally avoid eating root vegetables because tiny organisms are injured when the plant is pulled up and because a bulb or tuber's ability to sprout is seen as characteristic of a living being. Some Jains, considering that plants suffer too, will eat only fruits and legumes. They are not, however, vegans. Drinking the milk of a cow, which is to them sacred, is akin to drinking mother's milk: in this case, the milk of a sacred mother.

* * *

Preconceptions about "the other" do not end with humans of another culture. My fear of some animals, particularly large ones such as cows and horses, not to mention lions, stems largely from my ignorance of how they function – how they think or feel.

Little by little, our assumptions about the animal world are breaking down. A multi-disciplinary panel of speakers on BBC Radio 3's Freethinking programme surprisingly agreed at the outset of their discussion that there is no fundamental difference between human and nonhuman animals. Humanity is just one of the species that inhabit the planet. One speaker said that this question has been under discussion by philosophers for centuries and generally, whatever quality or ability is chosen for discussion, it is found that some individual animals have it and some humans do not.

Those who live or work with a particular species for many years are able to demonstrate that even characteristics that man has claimed as unique to our species, such as tool-making and thinking ahead, can be found in them. Frans de Waal has worked extensively with other primates such as chimps and bonobos, with a particular emphasis on empathy and peace-making. Even after acts of violence and aggression, which we more readily associate with this species, chimps can be found to be reconciled, consoling each other and exercising reciprocity, even displaying a sense of fairness. Similarities between humans and other primates were vividly exhibited in 2015/16 by dozens of questions covering an entire wall of the Wellcome collection (Marcus Coates, *Shared traits of the Hominini*), including: Are you absent-minded? Are you tender? Do you eat soil? Are you irrational? Do you vary your sexual positions?

But it is not enough to judge nonhuman animals according to human principles. The Dominican Matthew Fox frequently refers to his dog as his spiritual director. He is, as he says, being only partly facetious, considering that animals have a great deal to teach us: their joy in life, their playfulness sensitivity to mood, beauty and the power of non-verbal communication. Most of all, perhaps, in their ability to be present. They are as they are. Above all, we can admire the sheer "isness" of animals and the rest of creation, unhampered, as they are, by the weight of human self-consciousness. In nonhuman animals we have before us examples of effortless being.

Shared characteristics do not stop at the behavioural level, but stem from our genetic similarities. As Rutherford says, we share 99% of our DNA with other primates such as chimps and bonobos, but even in distantly related species, thousands of our genes are very similar. "DNA is the same in all species...That pathway retracing our steps as they become fainter and fainter over time, can be applied to any creature alive today, or ever." It is breath-taking to read that "in every cell is a perfect unbroken chain that stretches inevitably back to the origin of life" (45).

As we become more aware not only of the qualities and abilities of our fellow creatures, but the deep connections which bind us, question marks increasingly arise over many of our interactions with the nonhuman animal world. What do we think about horse racing? Horse riding? Going further, should we reconsider our domestication of animals? Our keeping of pets? In all these relationships, which keep animals in an artificial state of submission to the will of human beings, we are not treating them as equals; we cannot be said to be allowing them autonomy. We are still imposing our power of life and death. We need to move further along the spectrum from dominion to shared creatureliness, and share our lives at a deeper level. We need, as Thomas Berry says, to connect our "inner presence to other modes of being" (41).

I recently spent a week on Canna, one of Scotland's Little Isles, an island of some twenty human residents plus a few visitors staying on the island or on yachts moored in the bay. There are also about a hundred cattle, a thousand sheep and tens of thousands of sea birds. In such circumstances, the nonhuman population acquires a greater prominence. Staying there, being in such a minority as a human, shifted my perspective.

As Les and Pauline Mitchell wrote in their introduction to *Living by voices we shall never hear*:

We live in the midst of animals; the products of their bodies and products made from their bodies are everywhere. Over thousands of years we have used these beings for our own ends; for hauling loads, grinding grain, making roads, carrying people, working in mines, powering machinery, ploughing land and making war. each day of the year we kill, on average, in the food industry alone, the same number of animals as there are people in the whole of southern Africa. Animals have been our unpaid, unacknowledged and, for the most part, appallingly treated slaves, on whose backs, it is no exaggeration to say, our present world has been built. Perhaps it is time to consider our relationship with them.

6

Humans and the earth

And whilst you are contemplating the humble majesty of a blade of grass, with a spatial extent of a few centimeters but stretching back in the temporal direction for almost a third of the age of the Universe, pause for a moment to consider the viewer, because what is true of the blade of grass is also true for you. You share the same basic biochemistry... and much of the same genetic history, carefully documented in your DNA. This is because you share the same common ancestor. You are all related. You were once the same.

(Cox, *Wonders of Life*)

We are discovering that DNA not only connects us to those we have considered "other" among the human population, not only to nonhuman animals, *but to non-animals too.* Hard to believe, but the human body and the earth's crust have much the same chemical composition. We, like the earth, are mostly made up of water and a few core elements, including potassium, chlorine, magnesium and iron. Scientists from many disciplines are now finding evidence to support what most indigenous peoples have known and many faiths have understood for centuries. It is not them and us. We can't separate ourselves from the rest of creation.

According to the Oxford English Dictionary, ecology is the study of "the mutual relations of organisms with their environment". We need to remember that we are one of those organisms: it is our relation with our environment that we are looking at; we are part of the object of our study. Or, rather, as Thomas Berry says, we are part of "a communion of subjects not a collection of objects" (17).

The Buddhist principle of the oneness of self and environment (*esho funi*) means that life (*sho*) and its environment (*e*) are inseparable (*funi*). *Funi* means "two but not two" (www.sgi.org/).

This means that although we perceive things around us as separate from us, there is a dimension of our lives that is one with the universe. When we are grounded in the Spirit, we can have a sense of that utter oneness and mutuality with all that is: the animals, plants, the earth itself. The mutuality, the interdependence, of species is evident in every tiny detail of the lives of millions of plants and animals. Whether with a spiritual or a scientific understanding, we now know that at the most fundamental level of life itself, there is no separation between ourselves and the environment.

As with animals, those who spend time with different beings have a greater understanding of their intrinsic nature. Peter Wohlleben, who has spent most of his working life among forest trees, questions the difference in our attitudes to animal and plant life, saying that

the distinction between plant and animal is, after all, arbitrary and depends on the way an organism feeds itself: the former photosynthesises and the latter eats other living beings. Finally, the only other big difference is the amount of time it takes to process information and translate it into action (84).

He goes on to say that when we know more about the capabilities of vegetative beings and their emotional needs and lives, then we will treat plants in a different way.

And so to the earth itself. We do not own the earth. We cannot actually own land, though we think we do. People close to the land do not underestimate the quality of its being. John Todd of the New Alchemy Institute, who says, "I've been in love with the

Earth's living mantle since I was a small child", conducted an experiment with some friends. In their attempt to "create a commune where we could come into harmony with the earth", he and his colleagues realised that they needed to understand what was going on in their piece of land. Each person had to study one aspect of the place and share it with the others. "One after another we began to become sensitive to this particular place and it changed us; I don't think any of us has ever been the same since." One realisation was that in order to grasp anything a reduction in scale was necessary: "a reduction of the scale of our being to the point that we can grasp tangible wholes" (Katz *et al.*, 177, 178). In order to understand our planet home, we need to notice what is going on, to observe the details of other life, and respect them.

And while we have to remember that the rest of the created world is not there solely for the use of humankind, we need to recognise and be grateful for the fact that many aspects of our planet do benefit us hugely. According to the UK National Ecosystem Assessment, the UN recognises four basic categories of ecosystem service that nature provides to humanity:

- Provisioning - providing timber, wheat, fish, etc
- Regulating - disposing of pollutants, regulating rainfall, storing carbon
- Cultural - sacred sites, tourism, enjoyment of countryside and
- Supporting - maintaining soils and plant growth.

So, what are we doing in recognition of those benefits?

I believe that any consideration of our responsibility to the earth should begin in celebration. If we glory in the fullness of the magnificent gift of life in all its forms, how could we not want to protect it? Some years ago, wishing to challenge myself, I went to a workshop on the impact of our lifestyles on the environment.

As we went round the table, each contribution was gloomier than the last, ending with "well, maybe we should just stop breathing". Then, at last, a splendid young man in dreadlocks spoke passionately about the beauty of the created world, the glory of what we had been given - and the energy in the room lifted.

There are few of us who are not drawn to the beauty of the natural world. That is the gift to us of a bird, a flower or a tree: their presence invites a response which confirms the connection between us. Although I am a city woman, born and bred, the natural world has always been important to me - the birds, the stars, the elemental landscapes of mountains and the sea. During my year of travel, as I spent time in the desert and in rain forests, in snow and in tropical heat, it became a more and more important part of my reality. To unite with that of God in all creation was an irresistible pull. In Peru, we stayed in a three-sided house, one side open to the natural world. The sight of the Andes dominated my waking every morning, and penetrated my being. It was not a dualistic admiration of something external but a call to something within me. I had felt it in the desert, and now it was as if a magnet had entered my soul.

We have been given life. The scale and scope, the sheer diversity of the created world, is the context of that life. Awe and wonder and celebration of our earthly home are a natural response.

Climate change

The publication of Rachel Carson's *The Silent Spring* in 1962 was ground-breaking. Although its prime focus was on the impact of pesticides on the natural world, its impact went way beyond its original intention. It led to the founding of the Environmental Protection Agency in the United States, and was a forerunner of a number of influential books by ecologists, scientists and theologians on the deep connection between humanity and rest of the natural world, and the destructive impact of some human behaviour.

Although there are differences of opinion about the extent of human responsibility, climate change has become a matter of international concern. It may only have come to the forefront of mainstream thought in the last fifty years or so, but many cultures were alert to the dangers many years before. Most indigenous peoples, from Native Americans to African tribes, have long understood that any behaviour that interferes with any element, any being, in our web of connectedness, is bound to have a domino effect.

Bernie Krause (quoting Frank Keim) gives the melting of river ice as an example.

At the base of the ice there's an awful lot of algae, and the algae begin to bloom. With the blooming of the algae, the crustaceans – like copepods – eat the algae. The fish eat the crustaceans. The seals eat the fish. And then, of course, the polar bear and humans eat the seals. If the ice doesn't exist – and it's quickly disappearing because of global warming – if you don't have the ice, you don't have any of that (233).

Even if we are beginning to understand the effects of our behaviour, old habits die hard. We still despoil the earth with equanimity. We pollute the earth, the sea, the air and even space. We plant flags at the North Pole and fight over mineral deposits at the bottom of the sea. Even at the most basic level, the interference of humankind has had an impact. What we discover about the delicate interweavings and mutual necessity of different species is that they are at their purest state among wild animals and ancient forests. Our modern world with its domesticated and captive animals and planted, managed trees has had a powerful and detrimental impact on that balance. Planted trees behave more as individuals and, unsupported by a community, have shorter lives.

In books such as *The Earth After Us*, the geologist, Professor Jan Zalasiewicz, considers our impact on a much bigger scale, looking at what might be the legacy of humanity. He and his colleagues have estimated the extent of what they term the technosphere, which includes all that humankind has made, built, and produced, including its waste. It seems that the sum total of all that man has done, what we might call our marker on the planet, might add up to a weight of some thirty trillion tons, forming a layer round the planet of some half a metre thick. Our impact, he says, has been on a planetary scale, and is not always as much under our control as we think it is.

Sustainability

"Sustainability" is a word much bandied about, without much understanding of its meaning. The 1987 UN Bruntland Report defines it as "meeting the needs of the present generation without compromising the ability of future generations to meet their own needs". Only when our own physical or economic wellbeing is threatened, it seems, do we begin to take notice. Even when considering climate change or pollution, we tend to express our concern in terms of their effect on human beings (and sometimes animals). We take little account of the respect due to the earth for its own sake. We need to consider other elements of the universe as independent entities. Objections to GM crops or fracking should not just be because of their possible impact on human beings, but out of a consideration for the natural order. And the fact that these are only the latest examples of human interference is no reason for acceptance. Quite the contrary. Hybrid plants, selective breeding - we have a long way to go in changing our attitudes and behaviour.

It's not just about us. We need to modify our behaviour not for our own gain and protection, but because of a sense of responsibility to the rest of creation. We need to consider not just future generations of human beings, but that of the planet itself. As we learn more about the interconnectedness of the natural world, we need to acknowledge our true place as one among equals. At an international gathering of Quakers in Peru in 2016, it was recorded:

> We see that our misuse of the Earth's resources creates inequality, destroys community, affects health and well-being, leads to war and erodes our integrity.... We love this world as God's gift to us all. Our hearts are crying for our beloved mother Earth, who is sick and in need of our care.

It is easy, as we experience drought in some countries, floods in others, hear of the melting of the ice-caps, the danger to animal life because of change in habitat and shortage of foodstuff, to be swamped by the magnitude of the problem.

The matter is huge, and complex. We need to recognise that everything we do, every small thing, affects others, affects the universe, and that it is in those small everyday choices in our shopping, in the way we live our lives, that we express our faithfulness, and an understanding of our interdependence. There needs to be an incremental change in our own behaviour - including an acceptance that we are part of the problem.

No one says change is easy. We are surrounded by difficult choices. Take, for instance, the advice to eat locally sourced food. On visits to countries such as Costa Rica and Nicaragua, I saw how local people depended on markets created by Europe and the USA. If we stopped buying their bananas or coffee, many small farmers would be ruined. A change in our shopping habits is not enough; it needs to be accompanied by a radical re-alignment of world markets. What is needed is not a tinkering at the edges, but a fundamental shift in human behaviour. And that shift needs to be in recognition of our place in the universe, and our innate dependence on it. Instead of trying to exert our power over the rest of creation, we need to cherish the earth as the source of life, nurturing and sustaining humankind and the rest of the natural world, fostering growth and fertility. Mother Earth is a concept deep in folk history and common to the traditional peoples all over the world. We have lost touch with the relationships that matter. "The destruction of the planet", says Thomas Berry, "can be seen as a direct result of the loss of this capacity for human presence to and reciprocity with the nonhuman world" (18).

And of course our interconnectedness does not end with our own planet. Without our sun there would be no life on earth; without our moon, there would be no tides. Who knows what impact other suns, moons, planets and stars may have on us. We belong to something on an unimaginably vast scale: one trillion galaxies with an eighteen-billion-year history. As Martin Buber says, "We live our lives inscrutably included within the streaming mutual life of the universe."

Balance

The reality of the nonhuman animal world, as well as the human one, is that nature is not always benign. The food chain is part of the mutuality. But we know that killing can be for dominance as well as for food. Phrases abound about the violence of the nonhuman animal world: "the law of the jungle", "red in tooth and claw", "survival of the fittest". Whether referring to human or non-human animals, our connections exist *whether we like it or not*. It is not about approval, just recognition of the fact. It's easy to feel part of a group of like-minded individuals. It may feel possible that we are connected to a panda, a dog or a horse. It's not so easy with people we find difficult, tiresome or threatening. It's not so easy to feel connected to a mosquito or a crocodile. However we might disagree, dislike poison ivy, a cockroach or each other, we are all related and mutually dependent.

Every organism has its own interests. For most species any connection between them and another is for good or ill. Microbes, for instance, depending on the context or individual type, can have an either adverse or beneficial effect. The relationship between plants of different species can be mutually beneficial, one-sided, or parasitic. For some beings, and especially humans, there is a choice in how we behave.

In recent years a more integrated approach to biological research has led to a shift in our prevailing view of the natural world. From considering nature predominantly as a field of conflict we have moved to an understanding of a more co-operative world. Before us now is a picture of a co-operative, cyclic universe, an intricate web of mutually beneficial organisms.

Peter Wohlleben is sceptical about any entirely co-operative view of Nature.

Out there, under the trees, the law of the jungle rules. Every species wants to survive, and each takes from the others what it needs. All are basically ruthless, and the only reason every-thing doesn't collapse is because there are safeguards against those who demand more than their due. And one final limitation is an organism's own genetics: an organism that is too greedy and takes too much without giving anything in return destroys what it needs for life and dies out. Most species, therefore, have developed innate behaviours that protect the forest from overexploitation (113).

For "the forest" we might substitute "the planet". Wohlleben has an unexpectedly even-handed view of the balance needed between selfish and co-operative behaviour of living beings. Talking of felling trees to burn logs for our fires, he asks whether the fact that we are killing a living organism for our purposes is reprehensible. Despite having spent most of his working life among trees, he acknowledges that we, like other animals, are made in such a way that we can survive only with the help of organic substances from other species. The essential thing, he feels, is that we don't take more than is necessary from the forest ecosystem, and that we avoid unnecessary suffering in the process.

Wohlleben's view is that it is a matter of balance: that all have to look after their own interests but be fair to others; we might want to consider where the balance lies for humankind. Do we, to use his phrase "demand more than our due"? The impact of human activity on earth, the disappearance of thousands of species and the threat to many more, seems to indicate that we do.

Perhaps we will only be moved if we believe that our own lives are threatened by our behaviour. Matthew Fox asks us to consider "the price our species pays for resisting community or destroying those that have it" (2000:86). It has taken me a long time to understand that statements in the Old Testament such as "visiting the iniquity of the fathers on the children and the children's children, to the third and the fourth generation" (Exodus 34:6-7; Deuteronomy 5:8-10), are not meant to imply the actions of an externally vengeful God, but a statement of fact. What we do will have an impact on future generations: the result is implicit in the act.

There are signs that climate change, holes in the ozone layer and the melting of Arctic ice are bringing us to our senses. All we can do, perhaps, is heal some of the damage that we have done and guard against doing more. Even though we are increasingly conscious of the impact of human behaviour, we are less aware, maybe, of the resilience of the planet, of the healing mechanisms hidden in the web of connection that is our earth. As Fox says, "Creation itself will struggle for a balance and harmony even if humankind refuses to do so" (1983:296). Maybe, in the end, the earth will survive our destructive behaviour. Maybe, like the dinosaurs, it's just the humans that will die out.

7

Another dimension: beyond fairness

Infinite sharing is the law of God's inner life. He has made the sharing of ourselves the law of our own being, so that it is in loving others that we best love ourselves
(Merton 1996:1)

Yong speaks on behalf of microbes, Wohlleben for trees, but both writers are giving out the same message, a message that extends way beyond the field of either of them: that all of life is connected. Through scientific proof, the much earlier understandings of the indigenous peoples of the world, and from our own observation, we learn of the oneness of the natural world, of the mutuality and interdependence of all beings. What should be the response of humanity to this? Wohlleben talks of balance and fairness, of not taking more than our due. But is that enough?

The question of altruism has puzzled scientists from Darwin onwards. As biologists asked what advantage might accrue from altruistic behaviour, it was recognised that in kin relationships altruistic acts allow an individual to increase the success of its genes by helping relatives that share those genes. Where altruism involves unrelated individuals, there might be some expectation of reciprocity.

But altruism, generosity, self-sacrifice is not always so easily, so pragmatically, explained. The pattern of snow geese flying in a V formation is familiar as an example of co-operation, enabling them to take advantage of the aerodynamic effects of flying behind another bird. Less known, perhaps, is the fact that birds take turns at the front despite the fact that there is no obvious benefit to the individual. And altruism such as this is not limited to behaviour within a single species.

There are ample examples of animals of different species befriending each other, from sentimental pictures on Facebook of, for instance, an owl and a dog, to extraordinary stories in the rather more solemn pages of the National Geographic – of an iguana and a cat or a tortoise and a hippopotamus! Such unlikely friendships, it seems, can stem from the need for bonding among animals in captivity, or the loss of a parent or baby. Little is known of how nonhuman animals experience emotions, but it seems increasingly acceptable for scientists to talk, for instance, about empathy among animals.

Dolphins support sick or injured animals; birds alert others to the approach of a predator, even if it calls attention to themselves. It is startling to realise that, as a speaker on BBC radio's Cosmic Quest said, "To let us live, millions of stars have had to die" (102). Empathy, altruism and, in some cases, self-sacrifice.

If we simply accept altruism as part of the structure of the universe, we might question our own part in it. Whatever the similarities between human and other beings, however little we know of the emotional or conscious lives of other beings, we know that as humans we are aware of ourselves and our place in the world; we have a well-developed moral sense and a sophisticated imagination. We have choices. If generosity happens among other beings, how much more might we expect from humans? The advanced consciousness of humans brings responsibilities.

If we are so close a relation of all human beings, do we not wish to respond in love and a sense of community? If we are also in close relation to all nonhuman beings not only through what they give us but in our very DNA, isn't a proper response similarly one of love and appreciation of our kinship? Do we not, in celebration, awe and gratitude, wish to respond to the gifts and grace in the rest of the created world with our own generosity? As Matthew Fox has written, "Interdependence... is the basic consciousness of compassion (1983:280)."

And on an hourly basis, in every part of the world, that expectation is fulfilled. Human behaviour is full of stories of selflessness, compassion and generosity. Just the other day the winner of a prestigious art prize decided to share her winnings with the other finalists. The Metro newspaper carries a daily column in which contributors thank strangers who have come to their aid when they have lost their money, fallen ill, or got lost.

For a number of years I've been involved in setting up microcredit programmes in various parts of the world. This form of lending small amounts of money is to enable women in poverty to start their own businesses, and depends on the common bond of the group. They provide support for each other and guarantee each other's loans. If one member of a group falls ill or dies, it is usual for the others to repay the loan.

It is natural human behaviour to help others. People put others first, even to the extent of risking their own lives. Someone giving their kidney for a stranger, for instance; or trying to rescue someone in danger of drowning; or sheltering Jews from the Nazis. The reason that the obverse is news is because it is shocking and unexpected. Kindness is ordinary. It's not news.

The level of charitable donations and volunteering, the numbers attending demonstrations for social justice, are witness to a wish to make things better. It's easy to sink into the despair of those who gave me advice as a child: that the problems of the world - the poverty, the injustice - are all too big. I believe that many people would like to make a difference, but most have succumbed to the prevalent hopelessness. They simply don't know where to start or what to do.

Our response needs to come from an affirmation that our connection is not merely practical and utilitarian but, as indigenous peoples have understood for centuries, spiritual and deserving of a response from our deepest self. We are talking about another dimension. Science, as my microbiologist nephew remarked, is a focus on the particular. Religion opens our hearts to the infinite and eternal.

So, faced with all the poverty, all the injustice in the world, what can we do? The first thing is to recognise that there is no such thing as a small piece of work. As Mother Teresa said, "To God there is nothing small. The moment we have given it to God, it becomes infinite. (www.idlehearts,com). And we never know what seeds we sow.

We have to try not to be overwhelmed. All we can do and are, I believe, asked to do, is inform ourselves and to foster love in our hearts and actions. Become the person we are meant to be and fulfil our unique role in the world. What that call is for each of us to find out, to devote enough time listening to the guidance of the inner voice. No individual can do it all. Each of us will be drawn to different ways of working, different causes and groups. For some it will be mainly in prayer, for others in political campaigning or front-line action. Areas of work might include. mental health, animals, children, old age, marginalised groups such as prisoners or asylum seekers. or our own neighbourhood. As Frederick Buechner says: "The place God calls you to is the place where your deep gladness and the world's deep hunger meet" (Wishful Thinking: A Seeker's ABC, 118) Not duty, performed with a sigh, but something that speaks to and from our deepest self.

8

One in ourselves

Buddhism regards life as the unity of the physical and the spiritual. It
views all things, whether material or spiritual, seen or unseen, as
manifestations of the same ultimate universal law or source of life...
The physical and spiritual aspects of our lives are completely
inseparable and of equal importance.
(*SGI Quarterly*, April 1999)

There has been a tendency in Christianity for the body to be held
in less regard than the mind or the spirit. Other religions have a
more holistic approach, considering that our faith encompasses
the whole of our human selves. We are embodied. The incar-
nation in several religions teaches us of the inseparability of
matter and spirit: our wholeness, integrity, groundedness are a
crucial expression of who we are, and our connection with the
earth. Spirit without matter is as unbalanced as matter without
spirit, or materialism.

In all religions, body language is part of worship: a hand on
the heart, prostration, a sign of the cross, bringing hands together
in the classic prayer position. Even shutting our eyes, slowing our
breath and listening to our heartbeat can be part of our atten-
tiveness. Attention to our bodies is essential for our spiritual life.
Our bodies help us be more available to God through openness,
alertness and interior stillness. Posture, movement, gesture and
diet can all help us. And breath. Breathing exercises are central in
many traditions. Indeed, the name of God, pronounced in
Hebrew without consonants, is a breath, as is the name Allah.

When we consider the physical complexity of our bodies - the
millions of cells, bones, muscles and organs - the co-ordination of
our bodies is remarkable. When something goes wrong – we

break a leg or have a chest infection – it does affect the rest of the body, but that body miraculously adjusts. It is extraordinary how, at any given moment, how much of our body *is* working!

We have no problem in recognising the connectedness of different parts of our body:

Hip bone connected to the back bone
Back bone connected to the shoulder bone
Shoulder bone connected to the neck bone
Neck bone connected to the head bone
Now hear the word of the Lord.

That connectedness and, even more, the concept of each part of the body as a microcosm is at the heart of complementary therapies such as iridology or reflexology, in which the study of one part of the body can give us an insight into the condition of the whole. Medical specialisms that look at individual symptoms of an isolated part of the body are denying these connections, ignoring what can be learnt from a more holistic approach. Just as there is unity at the core of the created world, so there is in each individual. If in our history and physiology we are connected to, for instance, a rock or a carrot, how much more connection there is between apparently disparate parts of our bodies – a finger nail, for instance, and a hip joint. Although made up of different types of cells, they are contained in the same skin and connected by the same blood. According to the geneticist Adam Rutherford, "Every type of cell is a highly specialised member of a community, working in unison with others to build a fully functional organism" (9-10).

Each individual is unique – and complex. I know that there are many aspects to my being, some of which I may not like. I can perceive differently and behave differently with different people and at different times; there are different versions of each of us expressed in the different contexts of our lives. Peer pressure can have unpredictable results. The influence of others can lead us to behave in ways normally foreign to us. In a crowd, our behaviour might change significantly. In protest marches there can be solidarity but, as the adrenalin rises, there can also be tension.

Before we can be one with creation, we must reach oneness with our true nature. Who we are is the very foundation of our experience and perception of the universe (Anadi).

Who are we? Is there any such thing as the essential self? Or is it just the Self, the Divine, in us? Being in tune with the essence that others recognise in us.

How do we become one in ourselves? Maybe in the same way as we become one with others: in acceptance of difference, compassion with difficulty, being at home to ourselves, practising what John O'Donohue calls "inner hospitality". Being at one in ourselves and being at one with the world around us are part of the same process. As Thomas Berry writes: "Nothing can be itself without being in communion with everything else, nor can anything truly be the other without first acquiring a capacity for interior presence to itself" (quoted in Fox 1983:287).

That interior presence is hard to acquire. Living within ourselves requires allowing enough space for grace, for the Spirit, to enter in. It requires finding a way of life that encompasses a regular time to be still, to collect, gather, centre ourselves, bring the whole of ourselves into a state of awareness. I like the suggestion "Between actions, pause and *remember who you are.*" This is about collecting ourselves, bringing ourselves into a place of unity. "Re-member" is the opposite of "dismember". In the busiest of lives, we can find times – waiting at a bus stop, going upstairs – to stop our busy minds and remember who we are.

We hold within ourselves a series of balances: of practice and grace, of Light and dark, of the life within and the outside world; inner experience and outward witness; humility and using our full potential; being passive to God and active to the world; concentration on the present moment and with a view to the far horizon; time in eternity; this place in infinity. Joy and suffering; love and detachment; plenitude and the void (Kavanagh 2004).

Living that balance, holding the tension between longing and belonging, is the core of a unified life.

9

Unity

The relationship between the human and the divine; the heavenly and earthly spheres, is one of interdependence. The spirits "need" us, just as we "need" them; just as spirit "needs" matter to give it form, and matter "needs" spirit to give it force, being and reality.
(Dona Marimba Richards, in Fox 2000:91)

We live in a world with many religions. There is a rich diversity in practice, tradition and belief, and each owes the others respect. Since the major religions are committed to love and service to all, conflict between them is a travesty of their common purpose and often stems not from religion at all but from politics, nationalism and a quest for power. Exclusivity, throwing up barriers, would again seem a contradiction of any stated aim of universal love. The French mystic Simone Weil was a deeply committed Christian, but she refused to be baptised, refused to join the church. Her refusal was not from lack of faith and not only because of her feelings of unworthiness but because of the church's unwillingness to include non-believers, those who lived before Christ and those of other faiths.

Differences, and sometimes conflict, arise more often between the liberal and fundamentalist wings of religion than between specific religious faiths. Most importantly, at the mystic level all the major religions experience a profound commonality. When the focus is on a direct experience of and relationship with God, differences dissolve.

The commonality of faiths at this level has been expressed by many spiritual writers. F.C. Happold's *Mysticism* brings together writings from all traditions; Aldous Huxley gave a name to this common core in the title of his seminal *The Perennial Philosophy*.

Quakerism has its roots in Christianity but has always said that it is "open to new light". Now that there is more communication between faiths, so there is more "new light" available, but even at the beginning Quakers were aware of the unity at the source of all religion. In 1693 William Penn, with an extraordinarily modern consciousness, wrote:

> The humble, meek, merciful, just, pious, and devout souls are everywhere of one religion; and when death has taken off the mask they will know one another, though the divers liveries they wear here makes them strangers (*Quaker Faith & Practice*, 19:28).

The Benedictine Bede Griffiths echoes these sentiments when he asks:

> Where, then is this eternal religion...to be found? It is to be found in every religion as its ground or source, but it is beyond all formulation. It is the reality behind all rites, the truth behind all dogmas, the justice behind all laws. But it is also to be found in the heart of every man... It is not known by sense or reason but by the experience of the soul in its depths (98).

Elsewhere he writes that "all meditation should lead into silence, into the world of 'non-duality', when all the differences - and conflicts - in this world are transcended - not... simply annulled." He likens the deeper unity of being to "colours being absorbed into pure white light, which *contains* all the colours but resolves their differences" (Letter to Nigel Bruce, 1981).

How do we experience this oneness? How do we express it? Can we extend the collective consciousness that we sometimes experience in worship to how we are in the world? Can we tune into the Presence? In seeing that of God in everyone, can we make that connection? In just meeting someone's eyes we can both experience and express it. We can recognise then answer that of God in another. Not just acknowledging that there is that of God in each of us, but experiencing the connection and responding to it.

We have an impact on the world not only by what we do but in how we are, not only in doing, but in being. Remembering who are we are, and our connection with all that is, was and will be. Holding a sense of self in which past, present and all our possible selves are unified. Even alone, in prayer, there is power in our intention.

* * *

Every creature is a word of God (Eckhart)

"God" is a difficult word for many, but whatever word is used – Spirit, Light, the Divine - there are few who do not feel some sense of an over-arching power or force, both within and beyond. Many Native American tribes talk of "the great Spirit"; those who practise Buddhism - often defined in non-religious terms – sometimes use the word "source".

The other day I found myself humming this little ditty:

I'll sing you one, Ho
Green grow the rushes, Ho
What is your one, Ho?
One is one and all alone
And evermore shall be so.

When I looked it up, I discovered that the "one" in this ancient rhyme refers to God, the ultimate Oneness. The ultimate unity is not only in our experience of the Divine but the Divine itself. The One God is at the heart of all the major religions. Even religions like Hinduism which have a panoply of gods and goddesses explain that each is an expression of a part of the ultimate Divine.

All the richness and variety of the natural world is an expression of God. The Divine, manifest in both the most minute individual cell and the massive scale of the universe or even multiverses, is one: the unifying and connecting principle between and within all creation.

> Before we can realize oneness with creation, we must realize both oneness with our true self and with the source. The union of two unions – with our soul and with our source – is the base for arriving at universal transparency within which all of existence, both the uncreated and created, is embraced as one universal being. (Anadi)

Duality is a common mode for human beings: we define things by their opposites: light/dark, positive/negative. We separate subject and object, the observer and the observed. We identify ourselves with our different roles, as parent, colleague, writer, carer. In the spiritual life, all differences merge; opposites are held in unity. As the Jewish mystic, Martin Buber, explains, there are two kinds of experiences of non-duality. Just as in inner hospitality, our own collectedness can create a space from which to relate to others, so it is in the spiritual life. The soul itself needs to become a unity before it can achieve the second kind of unity, with what Anadi calls "the source". Buber talks of "living in the unfathomable nature of the relational act itself; in which two, it is imagined, become one" (86). He uses the words "it is imagined" as it is not expected that such an experience of ultimate unity is possible in an individual lifetime.

Most of us live an active life largely unconscious of the transcendental dimension. In general our attention is focused on the preoccupations of daily life, our consciousness punctuated only occasionally by withdrawal, a retreat, or a moment of self-remembrance. In periods of spiritual practice we may catch the occasional glimpse of something beyond, may even have what is referred to as a "peak experience", an enhanced perception of reality, when the boundaries between ourselves and the outside world are blurred, merged, when time vanishes and we feel the presence of the eternal in that moment, the infinite in that place. The oneness in all.

In his seminal *The Varieties of Religious Experience*, William James analyses peak experiences, and what they have in common. Over centuries, over different cultures and religions, peak experiences, it seems, have certain qualities in common. He found that they are "noetic" (i.e. have some content of knowing), that they are transient, that they are passive experiences, and that they bear some sense of unity – a breaking down of divisions and boundaries between the viewer and the viewed. All is one.

One such experience came to me during a workshop in Kent. It was when we were discussing the breaking down of boundaries, the merging of sensibilities, that I felt an overpowering recognition. The workshop leader said that when someone is asked to draw a tree, they usually begin by drawing their remembered concept of a tree, starting with the outline of a trunk, leaves and so on. But if they actually see clearly, feel one with the tree, they will indicate shade and colour quite differently, without boundaries. As he spoke of merging our sensibility with the tree, I felt such a merging quite powerfully. Drawn to the tree outside, I felt myself a part of it, at one. I at last understood why it is that I feel as I do in the desert: my soul *is* expanding into the space, out to touch the horizon. I am part of that space, one with it. The multitudinousness of the natural world was melted into the oneness of the Divine.

This feeling of unity was so powerful that I was quite overcome. I wept, sobbing with the intensity of the experience and with gratitude.

For most of us such an experience will be a rare and fleeting occurrence, but in his book on mysticism, F.C. Happold distinguishes a rare breed of human who have both the spiritual gifts and the complete commitment, who are not content with practising contemplation, but enter into a *state* of contemplation. In that state is found, he says, "a self-forgetting attention, a humble receptiveness, a still and steady gazing, an intense concentration, so that emotion, will, and thought are all fused and then lost in something that is none of them, but which embraces them all" (69-70).

Many writers have spoken of the contemplative experience:

Thomas Merton: "The contemplative is... one who, being perfectly unified in himself and recollected in the center of his own humility, enters into contact with reality by an immediacy that forgets the division between subject and object" (2013:151).

Matthew Fox: "That's mysticism: multiple experiences of unity. Mysticism is our unitive experiences - when you feel one with being, one with others, one with yourself, one with God" (Christ Path seminar, June 12, 2013).

Roswitha Jarman: "Mystic to me simply means allowing myself to sink deep into the holy unity of all and there to know this Unity and know the spirit experientially" (7).

However, it is not only through peak experiences that we can have an experience of the ineffable. We can feel it through the creative spirit gathering up all the richness of the human spirit as expressed in art, science, all our cultural achievements, past and present, which enrich our lives and create a precious thread running through humanity, shared even more widely in this age of global communication.

Earlier on we considered the efficacy of prayer. Among those who pray, whether for an individual or for world peace, there begins to grow an inner community and, at a more profound level, where prayer is more a state of being than a request for outcomes, what is expressed may come from a place of unity.

If you are abiding within the Self, there are no other people. You and I are the same. When I pray for you I pray for myself and when I pray for myself I pray for you. Real prayer is to abide within the Self...When you know the Self, the "I" "You" "He" and "She" disappear. They merge together in pure Consciousness. (Sri Ramana Maharshi)

As Christopher Goodchild says, "Prayer ... is a doorway into the oneness that permeates everything. This is the most sublime of all mysteries" (52).

The experience of each of us is unique, and if our understanding of God is based on experience, so too will be our expression of that understanding. Although I believe that to define God would be too diminish, distort the reality of something beyond human understanding, I can say that, for me, one experience of God is as the connecting, unifying principle. I experience God as the life-force, the spark of the Divine, not dualistically a creator, but immanent: the One manifest in the many. I experience God both in the uniqueness of living creatures - the birdness of a bird, the treeness of a tree - and in that which brings us together: the unifying and connecting principle between and within all creation, the movement in our hearts at the beauty of the natural world, the joy of recognition in the eyes of another human being. God as relationship.

How we live with that understanding is a constant challenge. Nouwen describes discernment as "hearing a deeper sound" beneath the noise of ordinary life, and "seeing through appearances" to the *interconnectedness* of all things, to gain a vision of how things hang together in our lives and in the world (176). Thomas Merton describes the contemplative life as "primarily a life of unity. A contemplative is one who has transcended divisions to reach a unity beyond division" (2013:147).

But it is not only in contemplation that that unity can be found. By seeking deeper meaning and purpose in our lives, we can tune into the universality of that quest. As Christopher Goodchild says,

When you understand it, when you really understand it, not just in your intellect, but in the bones of your being, that there is no separation between you and absolutely everything, which includes the divine, then the game changes. No longer are you swimming like a fish in the ocean of existence, going round and round in circles saying, "Where, O where is the ocean?" For now, you can see, and with ever greater clarity, that you and the ocean are one. There are clouds, for you are human, but the clouds no longer obscure the deeper reality of your true, timeless and unchanging nature. (14)

10

No other

One cold winter night, a group from a London charity were taking
drinks and sandwiches out to people sleeping on the streets. A woman,
perhaps in her fifties, in a skimpy cotton dress, asked for a blanket.
There were none to be had: the last had been given out, but a young
man some yards away called out, "She can have mine."
To the question "But what will you do?" he answered: "She needs it
more than I do. What's life about if you can't give a little love?"

What I learnt when I went on my first tea run for homeless people
on that evening over fifteen years ago was that *there is no such*
thing as "the other".

In one sense everyone else is the other, since each being is
unique. Each human being has a unique DNA, a unique combi-
nation of genes and cells. Why should we be surprised that each
snowflake is unique, when the fingerprints of no two people are
the same?

It is striking that when we are not familiar with members of
another tribe or animal species, we say that "they all look the
same". It is not only white Anglo-Saxons who are blinkered in
their vision. Other ethnic groups have similar problems in
finding distinguishing features in people of different races. In
Madagascar, I was told, "You *vazaha* (white people) all look the
same"; in Ghana: "you *obroni* (foreigners) all look the same".

As with human beings, generalising about a particular species
of nonhuman animal does not allow for the difference of
individual animals at different times and in different contexts.
Although we appreciate the individual characteristics of our pet
dog or cat, it is hard for most of us to tell one cow or sheep from
another. Only those that spend their life in caring for animals –

whether domesticated or wild - will be able to do so. Time spent with any being, human or otherwise, will enable us to distinguish the particularity, the uniqueness of that being.

Difference matters. Oneness is not sameness, and there is a difference between distinctiveness and separation. It's important to recognise not only what we have in common, but the difference that makes each of us unique. What we are talking about is respecting our diversity and from that position being at one. Each being has its place in the world, and our appreciation of that demands that we enable the autonomy of each.

In his book, *From the Bottom of the Pond*, the former Anglican priest, Simon Small, affirms the importance of diversity, quoting from Corinthians:

> For just as the body is one and has many members, and all the members of the body, though many, are one body, so it is with Christ...If the whole body were an eye, where would the hearing be? If the whole body were hearing where would the sense of smell be? (I Corinthians 12: vv 12 and 17)

And goes on to say:

> We have been given the gift of individuality. We are not called to be all the same...The flow of creation is an expansion from oneness to multiplicity, from uniformity to variety. Yet, this is not a random individuality, for each part is an essential part of a wholeness - and it is the whole which gives each part its meaning.

> Imagine an orchestra made up from many different kinds of musical instruments. An orchestra comprising only violins or clarinets would be incapable of all but the simplest music. A great symphony requires the different instruments of the orchestra to be different, fully, without holding back. It

requires the musicians to being their unique talents to bear in the service of the whole. Uniqueness and difference are shaped into something bigger than the sum of their parts...So it is with the spiritual life (Small, 35).

It sounds an impossible task for one unique being to connect with another, and yet we have such a strong sense of commonality, even with complete strangers, that we seek out what connects us and at different levels bathe in the glow of connection - with a stranger, a friend, or a lover. We need to belong.

From community to compassion

Community matters: in other species as well as our own. There is plenty of evidence of co-operation among individuals of many species, whether for the purposes of hunting or protection: lions, wolves and deer work in groups. Birds call warnings to each other; the grooming of monkeys is reciprocal. The natural world confirms that we are stronger in community.

A tree is not a forest. On its own, a tree cannot establish a consistent local climate. It is at the mercy of wind and weather. But together, many trees create an ecosystem that moderates extremes of heat and cold, stores a great deal of water, and generates a great deal of humidity. And in this protected environment, trees can live to be very old. To get to this point, the community must remain intact no matter what. (https://www.brainpickings.org/2016/09/26/the-hidden-life-of-trees-peter-wohlleben/)

A forest of trees, a group of animals, whether human or nonhuman, gains strength from its togetherness. And it is from a sense of our oneness, of the bonds of community, that we learn about kindness and compassion. So what does this mean in terms of how we live our lives?

In every field there arise examples of co-operation that we can build on. In organisations, instead of a hierarchy of power, a flatter structure in which the highest salary is no more than say four times the salary of the lowest-paid means a more equal share of the profits; co-operative ownership as in the John Lewis Partnership means that every employee has a sense of belonging. Similarly, in finance mutuality guards against excessive profits for the few, with all members given a vote in how the company is run. Building societies, credit unions and microcredit are run on co-operative lines.

Restorative justice takes account of all the people involved in a crime: the perpetrator, the victim and the community. Co-operative housing enables the sharing of resources and the kind of mutual support that extended families in other ages and other cultures have given each other. Emmaus, L'Arche and Camphill are all examples of communal living that is inclusive of homeless people or those with disabilities.

"Community" and "compassion" come from the same root ("com" = together), as do "kin" and "kindness". Together, one, related, we naturally respond to each other's needs. As a friend told me about living in a small row of houses: "We all look out for each other". And that can be true at a universal level. If we are all one, we know that inflicting pain on another is to harm ourselves. "Isolation and rugged individualism betray the very manner in which the universe operates" (Fox 2000:437) and can lead to the greed, selfishness and destructive behaviour of much of the consumer world. The Kingdom of Heaven or Republic of the Spirit is not made up of consumerism, competition and money-driven priorities, but of love, co-operation and community, recognising the common bond of all beings on the earth.

The one and the many[1]
We live in a world of dazzling profusion and diversity, and the

only way we can cope, come to terms with it, hold it in our heads, is by making divisions, separating things out one from another, classifying beings into species and genera, naming plants, animals, people, races, ages. But scientists warn that making arbitrary decisions about what something belongs to by "naming" it can lead to misleading information and artificial simplification.

We know that it is more generally true. We are culturally conditioned to think in discrete units. Simplification, labelling, can lead, as have seen, to assumptions and stereotyping of people we have artificially put into groups of whatever kind. As the commonality between all forms of life becomes more evident, our habit of categorisation and separation seems increasingly unhelpful. Whether talking about different species or different races of humankind, the overlap is far greater than we had thought.

It is interesting that when our memories start to fail, it is the names, not the verbs or the adjectives, that are the first to go. Do names matter? It was Romeo's self that Juliet loved, not his hated family name. "A rose by any other name", she said, "would smell as sweet."

We are not talking about blurring the boundaries between different people, or about over-identification one with another. Being cautious about categorising and separation is not to deny difference. In a lecture on empathy given in October 2016, the former Archbishop of Canterbury, Rowan Williams, emphasised that it is not enough to understand what we have in common: we also need to understand our differences. It isn't always appropriate to say "I understand what you are going through". We sometimes need to say "I don't understand what you are going through." Only when we take the time to understand a different culture might we begin to understand how someone feels in a certain situation. Connection does not preclude recognition of our difference.

As the Quaker, Harvey Gillman writes: "There are many ways of being human and that diversity is what we all have in common." We live with the glorious paradox that at the heart of the unimaginable diversity, complexity, richness of the universe or possibly of countless multiverses and all that is in them, there is oneness, unity.

Roswitha Jarman sums it up well:

In the outer world there is division and multiplicity, subject and object, point and counterpoint. There our reason and senses are active. In the inner world we understand about oneness – here we know ourselves as one with all, as part of the whole. (39)

But, as she says, as we live with and journey from the outer to the inner, we learn that there is no division there either: "we know from experience that the inner and the outer are one, that the whole of life is sacred" (*ibid.*).

* * *

From religion, in science, and from our own daily experience, we can see that separation and division are human distortions. We know that the universe is one and that any disturbance of any part of it will upset that fragile balance. The more we can recognise the oneness of all, the closer we will draw to the One from whom all emerges and in whom all meets. Oneness, unity, brings together all human beings, all of the created world, all religions, and, in those rare moments of revelation, they can be experienced in the oneness of the Divine.

There is no room for any concept of "the other". When times seem dark, and our web of connectedness frighteningly fragile, it is all the more important to hold fast to our core values of love and compassion and not give in to despair. We have to try not to be tempted into hatred or demonisation but to stand up for those under attack and be alongside those in pain, grief and loss. Now is the time to remember the strength of the human spirit, the resilience of the earth and the divine source of our unity. It is a time to remember that we are one, and to do what love requires of us.

Endnote

1 "The one and the many" is a sculpture in Fitzroy Place in central London: a massive granite boulder, inscribed with scripts and symbols from many of the world's languages, focusing on stories of creation, cosmology and the formation of the universe, illustrating, says the sculptor, Peter Randall-Page, the essence of creativity across many cultures.

Further reading

All page numbers in the text are for the following websites or editions:

http://anaditeaching.com/

Berry, Thomas, *Evening Thoughts*. San Francisco: Sahara Club books, 2006

Buber, Martin, *I and Thou*. Edinburgh: T&T Clark, 1947

Capra, Fritjof, Steindl-Rast, David, with Matus, Thomas, *Belonging to the Universe*. London: Penguin, 1992

Dale, Jonathan, (ed.), *Faith in Action*. London: Quaker Home Service, 2000

De Waal, Frans, *Are we Smart Enough to Know how Smart Animals are?* New York: Norton, 2016

Fox, Matthew, *Original Blessing*. Santa Fe: Bear & Co, 1983

One River, Many Wells. New York: Penguin Putnam, 2000

Goodchild, C., *Unclouded by Longing*. London: Jessica Kingsley, 2017

Griffiths, Bede, *Return to the Center*, Illinois: Templegate, 1977

Happold, F.C., *Mysticism*. Harmondsworth: Penguin, 1970

Jarman, Roswitha, *Breakthrough to Unity*. London: The Kindlers, 2010

Kavanagh, Jennifer, *Call of the Bell Bird*. London: Quaker Books, 2004 (available now as a free e-book)

Journey Home. Alresford, Hampshire: O Books, 2012

A little book of unknowing. Alresford, Hampshire: Christian Alternative Books,   2015

Krause, Bernie, *The Great Animal Orchestra*. London: Profile, 2013

Kumar, Satish, "Schumacher lecture", 30 October 2004

Merton. Thomas, *No Man is an Island*. Kent: Burns & Oats, 1996

The Inner Experience. London: SPCK, 2013

Mitchell, L and P, *Living by voices we shall never hear*.

Grahamstown, South Africa: NISC (Pty) Ltd, 2013

Nouwen, Henri, et al., *Discernment*. London: SPCK, 2013

O'Donohue, John, *Eternal Echoes*. NY: Bantam, 2000

Divine Beauty. NY: Bantam, 2004

Pearce, Patricia, *Huffington Post*, 7 July 2016.

Picket, Kate and Wilkinson, Richard, *The Spirit Level*. London: Allen Lane, 2009

Rutherford, Adam, *The Origins of Life*. London: Viking, 2013

Quaker Faith & Practice. London: Quaker Books; 5th Revised edition, 2013

www.sgi-uk.org

Small, Simon, *From the Bottom of the Pond*. Ropley, Hampshire: O-Books, 2007

Walsche, Neale Donald, *Home with God*. London: Hodder & Stoughton, 2006

Wohlleben, Peter, *The Hidden Life of Trees*. Vancouver: Greystone Books, 2016

Yong, Ed, *I Contain Multitudes*. London: The Bodley Head, 2016

About the author

Jennifer is one of the most interesting writers of our generation on spirituality.

Derek A. Collins, London Centre for Spirituality.

Jennifer Kavanagh worked in publishing for nearly thirty years, the last fourteen as an independent literary agent. In the past fifteen years she has run a community centre in London's East End, worked with street homeless people and refugees, and set up microcredit programmes in London and in Africa. She has also worked as a research associate for the Prison Reform Trust and currently facilitates workshops for conflict resolution both in prison and in the community. Jennifer contributes regularly to the Quaker press, and runs a variety of courses, often based on her writing. She has published seven previous books of non-fiction, and one novel, *The Emancipation of B.* She is a Churchill Fellow and a Fellow of the Royal Society of Arts.

Message from the author:

Thank you for reading *Heart of Oneness: a little book of connection.* I hope you enjoyed it. If you have a few moments, I'd be very grateful if you could put a short review on your favourite online site. If you would like to hear about books or courses coming up in the near future, please visit my website: www.jenniferka-vanagh.co.uk

Other Books by Jennifer Kavanagh you may enjoy

Journey Home

Home - one of the most emotive words in any language. But it can mean different things to different people and, based on extensive interviews, Jennifer Kavanagh explores our outer and inner identities and asks: "What does home mean to you?" Home is not just four walls or the country in which we were born. It is not a locked door, an investment, a legal address, or a nation with rigid borders. Home is where the heart is: a yearning for a precious past, a dream of something that has never been, or a present reality. In relationship – with our families, in community, and with the whole of creation. In this compelling and immensely readable book, Kavanagh suggests that we will never be at home unless we are at home to ourselves. Home is where we all want to be.

This book is important reading for anyone who would seek to explore the concept further. Terry Waite CBE.

A Little Book of Unknowing

What if the facts on which we base our lives are shown to be unreliable? What if our expectations are confounded? What if we let go of those assumptions and expectations? What if we let go of our familiar, habitual ways of thinking? What if we let go of the very need to know? Unknowing is at the centre of spiritual life. It is only by creating a space in which anything can happen that we allow God to speak; only by stepping back that we allow space for that unpredictable Spirit that brings us gifts beyond any of our imaginings.

An ancient approach to spiritual exploration, rediscovered for the modern age. An important book that will help many people. Rev Simon Small; Chaplain, Abbey House Retreat Centre, Glastonbury.

Simplicity Made Easy

In folk history and religion, from the Shakers to Zen, we see the importance of simplicity. The appeal of living more simply may be to leave a smaller carbon footprint, to express a compassionate solidarity with those who have least, or simply to downsize. Whatever our own motivation, it is likely to spring from within. At heart, simplicity is a focus on what matters. Reducing the clutter in our lives, whether in material objects or in use of time or money, leads to an increased clarity of vision. Step by step, we can move towards a state in which our attitudes and life are made one. Simplicity is the outward and visible sign of an inward and spiritual grace. Simplicity is more than a lifestyle option: it is a way of life.

CHRISTIAN
ALTERNATIVE

CHRISTIAN ALTERNATIVE

THE NEW OPEN SPACES

Throughout the two thousand years of Christian tradition there have been, and still are, groups and individuals that exist in the margins and upon the edge of faith. But in Christianity's contrapuntal history it has often been these outcasts and pioneers that have forged contemporary orthodoxy out of former radicalism as belief evolves to engage with and encompass the ever-changing social and scientific realities. Real faith lies not in the comfortable certainties of the Orthodox, but somewhere in a half-glimpsed hinterland on the dirt track to Emmaus, where the Death of God meets the Resurrection, where the supernatural Christ meets the historical Jesus, and where the revolution liberates both the oppressed and the oppressors.

Welcome to Christian Alternative... a space at the edge where the light shines through.
If you have enjoyed this book, why not tell other readers by posting a review on your preferred book site.

Recent bestsellers from Christian Alternative are:

Bread Not Stones
The Autobiography of An Eventful Life
Una Kroll
The spiritual autobiography of a truly remarkable woman and a
history of the struggle for ordination in the Church of England.
Paperback: 978-1-78279-804-0 ebook: 978-1-78279-805-7

The Quaker Way
A Rediscovery
Rex Ambler
Although fairly well known, Quakerism is not well understood.
The purpose of this book is to explain how Quakerism works as
a spiritual practice.
Paperback: 978-1-78099-657-8 ebook: 978-1-78099-658-5

Blue Sky God
The Evolution of Science and Christianity
Don MacGregor
Quantum consciousness, morphic fields and blue-sky
thinking about God and Jesus the Christ.
Paperback: 978-1-84694-937-1 ebook: 978-1-84694-938-8

Celtic Wheel of the Year
Tess Ward
An original and inspiring selection of prayers combining
Christian and Celtic Pagan traditions, and interweaving their
calendars into a single pattern of prayer for every morning
and night of the year.
Paperback: 978-1-90504-795-6

Christian Atheist
Belonging without Believing
Brian Mountford
Christian Atheists don't believe in God but miss him: especially
the transcendent beauty of his music, language, ethics, and
community.
Paperback: 978-1-84694-439-0 ebook: 978-1-84694-929-6

Compassion Or Apocalypse?
A Comprehensible Guide to the Thoughts of René Girard
James Warren
How René Girard changes the way we think about God and the
Bible, and its relevance for our apocalypse-threatened world.
Paperback: 978-1-78279-073-0 ebook: 978-1-78279-072-3

Diary Of A Gay Priest
The Tightrope Walker
Rev. Dr. Malcolm Johnson
Full of anecdotes and amusing stories, but the Church is still a
dangerous place for a gay priest.
Paperback: 978-1-78279-002-0 ebook: 978-1-78099-999-9

Do You Need God?
Exploring Different Paths to Spirituality Even For Atheists
Rory J.Q. Barnes
An unbiased guide to the building blocks of spiritual belief.
Paperback: 978-1-78279-380-9 ebook: 978-1-78279-379-3

The Gay Gospels
Good News for Lesbian, Gay, Bisexual, and Transgendered
People
Keith Sharpe
This book refutes the idea that the Bible is homophobic and
makes visible the gay lives and validated homoerotic
experience to be found in it.
Paperback: 978-1-84694-548-9 ebook: 978-1-78099-063-7

The Illusion of "Truth"
The Real Jesus Behind the Grand Myth
Thomas Nehrer
Nehrer, uniquely aware of Reality's integrated flow, elucidates
Jesus' penetrating, often mystifying insights – exposing
widespread religious, scholarly and skeptical fallacy.
Paperback: 978-1-78279-548-3 ebook: 978-1-78279-551-3

Do We Need God to be Good?
An Anthropologist Considers the Evidence
C.R. Hallpike
What anthropology shows us about the delusions of New
Atheism and Humanism.
Paperback: 978-1-78535-217-1 ebook: 978-1-78535-218-8

Fingerprints of Fire, Footprints of Peace
A Spiritual Manifesto from a Jesus Perspective
Noel Moules
Christian spirituality with attitude. Fourteen provocative
pictures, from Radical Mystic to Messianic Anarchist, that
explore identity, destiny, values and activism.
Paperback: 978-1-84694-612-7 ebook: 978-1-78099-903-6

Readers of ebooks can buy or view any of these bestsellers by clicking on the live link in the title. Most titles are published in paperback and as an ebook. Paperbacks are available in traditional bookshops. Both print and ebook formats are available online.

Find more titles and sign up to our readers' newsletter at http://www.johnhuntpublishing.com/christianity
Follow us on Facebook at
https://www.facebook.com/ChristianAlternative